On
Digestion

Writers in the *On Series*

Gay Bilson

On Digestion

hachette
AUSTRALIA

Published in Australia and New Zealand in 2020
by Hachette Australia
(an imprint of Hachette Australia Pty Limited)
Level 17, 207 Kent Street, Sydney NSW 2000
www.hachette.com.au

First published in 2008 by Melbourne University Publishing

10 9 8 7 6 5 4 3 2 1

A catalogue record for this
book is available from the
National Library of Australia

ISBN: 978 0 7336 4442 9 (paperback)

Original cover concept by Nada Backovic Design
Text design by Alice Graphics
Typeset by Typeskill
Printed and bound in Australia by McPherson's Printing Group

The paper this book is printed on is certified against the
Forest Stewardship Council® Standards. McPherson's Printing
Group holds FSC® chain of custody certification SA-COC-005379.
FSC® promotes environmentally responsible, socially beneficial
and economically viable management of the world's forests.

If the idea of stalking through the outback looking for bush tucker—bits of plants given reassuring Western names to assist in their digestion, such as 'bush tomato' or 'bush banana'—was your thing, you could go for it.

Paul Toohey, *Last Drinks*

Nibble

On the ground, under the 5-year-old pomegranate tree, are two plush red fruit. One has split. The membrane is showing on a small part of the other. The week before, fallen fruit showed beak marks but the casing defeated the marauding Eastern Rosellas who compete with me for apples, peaches and apricots and have now seen that there are quinces as well. By design, this fruit, the pomegranate, is all mine.

Now, early May, the tree still holds some thirty of them, so heavy, so pregnant with seeds that the slender, supple branches droop low. Most of the leaves have fallen, some yellowing ones are still attached, and there are even a few bright-green, red-tipped young shoots, the tree puzzling over shifting drought conditions in South Australia, the earth retaining warmth and so out of kilter with the calendar seasons, or possibly my injudicious, erratic, parsimonious watering, although this tree, of all the useful fruiting trees, grew productively through the frighteningly dry summer. Another pomegranate, less than a year old, a sucker from someone else's tree, has not noticed winter. Its leaves are still bright green and flowers are still forming. The ur-pomegranate is one of the many species whose origin is the Fertile Crescent, Afghanistan probably its starting point.

I have counted the seeds in pomegranates. I cut each fruit in half across its width to take the seeds from their tightly packed crevices. There are seven lines of seeds showing, the seventh always thinner, squashed, a runt, and the thick, yellowish, unpalatable pith is obvious. Then I halve each of these pieces. A little bright, clear, red juice is lost. I take each quarter, and peel back a part of the leathery skin to expose the seeds, which are easily detached. The membrane below is a marvel of indentation patterns where it has been pressed against each cache of seeds, which are faceted and flat against it. Always I am impressed by their abundance and one day guessed how many there might be, then counted. Guessing 200, perhaps more, the count came to more than 400: the gravid pomegranate.

At this time of year all the fruit is perfectly ripe, even splitting. The splits exaggerate the fecundity of the fruit, preposterously packed with bright seeds, shaped so perfectly for their tight fit, or is it the tight fit shaping them? There is a flat surface at the tip of the seed, making a sixth plane: jewels fashioned by evolution. In AS Byatt's novella *Morpho Eugenia*, set in the mid nineteenth century, the Rev. Harold Alabaster remarks to the naturalist and explorer William Adamson: 'It has been well argued that mystery is another name for matter—we are and have access to Mind, but Matter is mysterious in its very nature'.

Impatient, I had begun picking at the end of March, but this was far too early and the seeds were pink at most, all sour crunch and little juice. Still, scattered with crushed green pistachios, toasted, sliced almonds and crushed, dried, deep-burgundy, heavily scented rose petals on the surface of whipped cream smothering a trifle, they were pretty and shone.

Then, reading about pomegranate groves in Spain, I learned that the fruit ripens sequentially, a useful, culinary kindness, an extension of plenty. Why must I read a book to see what is under my nose? It is, perhaps, a form of corroboration, but even this showed a lack of imagination and horticultural timidity.

In the kitchen, via the garden, I am often torn between theory and praxis, when surely the latter is all that matters here. Yet the largest bench, the one dividing the dining area from the kitchen itself, is never used for culinary preparation. It is this surface which many Australian kitchens, including mine, feel they need, the one piled with books and journals, notepaper and pens, the surface where we are reinventing ourselves, constructing a different, self-conscious culinary tradition.

It is at this metaphorical bench that I think about food. Not so much the really big questions of climate change, drought, agriculture, unequal food supply and the strategies of the industrial food suppliers, but the intimate ones connected to cooking, feeding and home: the choices one might make, the uses for seasonal plenty, the most satisfying ways to use leftovers, how to rectify culinary mistakes, decisions about supply and storage, forethought and lists. In sum, the tactics of everyday life. But at this bench are different books and journals, those either unrelated to food or those about food but not practical instruction, which form the backbone of gastronomic education but do not necessarily improve your cooking.

How, for instance, do we answer Rachel Lauden's provocation, in an issue of the Boston-based journal *Gastronomica*, that 'we should love new, fast, processed food?' How counter her charge that we who shun what she calls Culinary Modernism are culinary luddites? Do we laugh or cry at the advertisement for a compact disc, 'a collaboration between two Australian artists', of contemporary music called *Slow Food* that includes in its package the recipe for the dish which is also the art on the cover? How might I reconcile gratitude and appreciation for the local farmers' market while mostly staying away because I don't like crowds? How might I make most imaginative use of incidental, literary references to food and dining in poetry and novels and not seem pretentious to those who think them irrelevant? How might we counteract the constant and superficial advertisement which is taken for writing about food? The most exact, economical praise of a dish I have ever read is 'passingly excellent', Ishmael's opinion about a clam chowder in Melville's *Moby-Dick*. How might we write about food with 'evocative exactitude' (the novelist John Banville's lovely phrase about a different subject altogether) leaving out the egregious and ubiquitous descriptions which all amount to the epithet 'delicious'? Indeed, there is something about food which seems to defy all attempts to explain the pleasure it gives us through flavour and aroma as well as to acknowledge its central, material role in our staying alive, making us who we are.

Food is both less and more than that. If we divide ways of communicating into speech and writing, then cookery is speech.

And how do we truly comprehend the price of food when so much is written about sharing and gift-making? In *Economy of the Unlost*, Anne Carson writes about Simonides, the first Western poet to take money for his poetry. Poetry might be said to be the most economical of literary forms, and also the most rigorous. To be a great poet is to have a gift. To be a truly great cook is to have a gift also. To cook simply and to share is to be involved in gift-making. There is a particular order of monks who will not take monetary payment for their singing or for the singing lessons they give. Instead, they will accept food as payment. In this way, people learn to cook in order to make music.

This bench, the bridge between the kitchen and the dining room, is the one where, turning away from the heat of the stove, I am drawn to different theories, speculations on digestion, ways of reconciling or not reconciling love of cookery and love of words, the first practical, ephemeral and sustaining, the second cerebral and lasting.

First Course

The antihero of John Lanchester's first, clever novel, *The Debt to Pleasure*, is a bore. He is an exaggerated, murderous version of the foodie, a term invented in 1984 by Paul Levy and Ann Barr in *The Official*

Foodie's Handbook to describe those who are obsessed with food. The 'foodie' jealously inhabits an exclusive domain and falls easily into distasteful, indigestible, culinary competitiveness. The word was coined at the height of an interest in nouvelle cuisine, the new French cooking, when culinary tourism began to include those particular French restaurants which became exclusive destinations. 'Foodie' is included in the 1993 edition of the *Oxford English Dictionary*. It is an ugly word, mostly used pejoratively, connoting greedy indulgence.

Lanchester's character is fictional, nasty, misanthropic and sly. His obsessive interest in food and cookery is coupled with a murderous dislike of people.

The foodie defined by Levy and Barr, and mercilessly satirised by Lanchester, was a product of an era when dining out was the measure by which you showed what you knew about food. If you were a foodie you made a booking, almost exclusively in French restaurants. Your relationship to good food was an expensive one.

Gastronomic life is more airy now. A much more digestible, far less exclusive but still often privileged interest in food is espoused by people who build their own wood-fired ovens, grow their own produce and sometimes write about it. If the foodie was once a version of a collector then now he has embraced engagement and dirties his hands. Roger Scholes' three-part documentary *The Passionate Apprentices*, shown on SBS television in 2008, follows three Tasmanians, a knife-maker, a beekeeper and a baker, as they work and teach and share their experience with much younger people. This gentle, celebratory documentary has an almost medieval air, embracing journeymen's trades. The knife-maker fittingly barters knives for food; the beekeeper's daughter, wide-eyed, interested, goes with her father to collect honey from the hives he places near far flowers; the baker knows his employee will use his skills in his own bakery one day. None of these people are building empires; all are connected to place. The only glitch is that the 'passionate' in the title is redundant, tautological. These artisans embody the Zen paradox of deserving the work but not the reward.

Despite little triumphs like this unpretentious celebration of skilled people who might still be misunderstood by much of mainstream society as feral outsiders, the broadsheet newspapers and the glossy magazines continue to insist on treating food not only as an infinite possibility for marketing but also as something divorced from agriculture, paying attention only to growers and artisans who supply precious crops to precious few. Serious, well-researched articles about land, water and scarcity are cordoned off in the editorial, environment and rural pages. Places like public hospitals, which feed large populations of patients, are left to the general and frightening malaise of their industrial foods. The interesting, troubling industrial food category called 'functional', defined by an expert at a food conference as including 'foods which have specific (and scientifically verified) health benefits and foods which include functional ingredients which provide better appearance, texture and mouthfeel', is never investigated by journalists in the food pages, which treat cooking and dining out as hobbies and as indigestible gossip. At that same conference, fishery representatives boasted that Australian waters have an enviable 'green' reputation, yet this reputation is exclusively developed towards increased exports. Fishermen who might sell their catch in situ find often that this is illegal. The food pages have certainly worked successfully to persuade regulators that cheeses like Roquefort and cured meat products like Iberico ham should be allowed into Australia, but both are so expensive, such a long-distance indulgence, that their importation has no effect whatsoever on the mainstream diet. It is not that there is anything wrong with writing about pleasure and taste, but there is such a disconnection between the marketed idea of good living and the ways and means of agricultural production and harvesting.

If you are a bookish sort of person then the bench which is never used for cooking might be the place where books about different food cultures make up for the segregation and superficiality of much of the food writing in the media, yet when recording a culinary culture, books offer only thin knowledge. Perhaps we might blame recipe books for the ever-increasing super-ficiality of our interest in food cultures? In the last thirty or so years they have been falling from the sky like the 'mobile food' from the fifteenth- and sixteenth-century Middle Dutch poems about Cockaigne and Luilekkerland ('lazy-luscious-land'), far-fetched imaginings particular to a society which experienced drastic hunger and overabundant surplus in many a cyclical almanac. In contemporary society there is a constant reinvention of dishes in the interests of new ownership—'this is my recipe now'—but food has a conservative habit and usually refuses to be transformed except by its outer garments and costume jewellery, which change with voguish regularity.

On this bench is Lilia Zaquali's *Medieval Cuisine in the Islamic World*. The dust jacket has a marvellous painting of pomegranates. Greedy for more pomegranate stories, because of the tree which provided so many, and knowing just enough about the combinations of ingredients in Middle Eastern and Persian cookery, of meat with fruit and nuts and spices, I found a recipe for chicken with pomegranate and walnuts.

This dish, *fesenjân*, requires fresh pomegranate juice. Richard Burton, the eighteenth-century English traveller and melancholic, wrote that he had found a pomegranate called a shami, 'almost stoneless, delicately perfumed and as large as an infant's head'. Apparently the people in some of the original pomegranate countries have always aspired to fruit which have virtually no 'stones' and are all juice, a trait I cannot imagine and have no reason to want as yet, for the enchantment with the matter which is a pomegranate and which is connected to every symbolic representation of the fruit is centred on the profusion of tightly packed seeds, Lorca's 'tiny beehive/with a bloodstained honeycomb'.

Yet for centuries we have been selectively breeding plants which are used as food so that they serve us better. Michael Pollan, in *The Botany of Desire*, suggests that the potato and the apple, for instance, have both benefited from our desire to improve them as food. The cultivated pomegranate might conceivably have no seeds at all— think of the navel orange. I cannot imagine it, but if I had not known the one with 400 seeds, the colour of the juice would be no less loud. In this house, after the initial seasonal delight of using the seeds with summer vegetables like eggplants, they have simply been added to yogurt in the morning (white and glistening red, shockingly symbolic), then turned to juice with the full harvest, along with the oranges, and 'squeezed' in the same way.

It is, perhaps, the perfection of combining the sweet with the savoury, fruit with meat, which is the seduction of Persian and North African dishes. Think of the legitimacy of the quince used as a baked or braised accompaniment to meats and of the sugar and cinnamon on the surface of *bisteeya*, the North African pigeon or chicken pie made with an interesting pastry called *warka*.

The last pomegranates hang so heavily on the almost bare tree in late autumn, directly in front of the kitchen window. Cultivating them, and so cultivating ourselves, we who are interested in food beyond nourishment are moved to know more and more, to turn from the garden, from the kitchen itself, to the bench with the books. And yet there is a slight discomfort with this need to know as much as I might know through reading, when experience and thoughtful practice would do.

Second Course

William Dalrymple has written about the extraordinarily long, orally transmitted poems which are still performed in the Indian state of Rajasthan. He met a Rajasthani princess who had determined to find a *bopha* (a storyteller) who was able to recite the entire Dev Narayan epic. She taped long sessions with the *bopha*. He sang while she wrote, sometimes for hours and hours at a time. She counted 626 pages of text which she had transcribed from the tapes she had made and which the *bopha* had sung from memory. The rani told Dalrymple that she thought the stories would die out: 'When the stories used to be told, everyone had a horse and some cattle … Now, when a *bopha* tells stories about the beauty of a horse, it doesn't make the same connection'. The stories were still alive in the particular part of Rajasthan that Dalrymple visited because 'the pastoral context of the story … was still intact'. As well, the Gujars (the herding class to which the god Dev Narayan belonged) are often illiterate, including the storytellers. With literacy, astonishing feats of memory are not needed. 'The illiterate have a capacity to remember in a way that the literate simply do not.'

A very large number of contemporary cookbooks are by professionals whose motive is not so much to impart knowledge as to show us who they are. These lavishly illustrated books are more biographical summary than shared information. This does not demean the recipes, but usefulness is not their paramount concern. Pictures are central to these books, not in order to illustrate technique but to show the chef's dishes at that point just before digestion. There is no narrative.

As a witty reaction to these picture-perfect books, *Nose to Tail Eating*, a collection of the British chef Fergus Henderson's recipes, published in 1999, eschewed perfection. The photographs are of table surfaces as the food is taken from central plates and is always partly consumed: greasy hands pulling meat from bones, food-encrusted forks, crumbs, and the jetsam of cracked shellfish littering the table. The photographs have an almost grubby air; things are a mess. The sense of activity in that truthful moment is intelligently captured, but they are still photographs, the table a stage. These are framed moments in a story which we will never know from beginning to end.

Behind the plethora of recipes to which we now have access is a narrative which is often as much construction as it is authentic. At a recent food and wine writers' festival, the chef Rick Stein told his rapt audience that, when making a television series about food in Mediterranean countries, he was in Sardinia with a camera crew, scouting for the locations, producers and cooks who would live up to what he wanted them to be. He interviewed the maker of a marvellous traditional dish of wild boar with mountain herbs, olive oil and potatoes. Asked what he would like to eat when he returned home from the wild terrain in which he was filmed, the man nominated smoked salmon roulade. Of course, we all speak in deference to our interlocutor and the cook was probably boasting of his knowledge of a sophisticated world outside his own, half serious, perhaps half sly.

At the same session Elizabeth Luard spoke about the way that recipes which have played a central part in the conservative culinary culture of a particular geographical place change once they have been written down by outsiders. Because of culling, choice and often compromise, daughters begin to cook their grandmothers' and mothers' recipes by the book (presumably sent back to the community by the acclaimed outsider in gratitude for cooperation and free labour) because this is how the outside world knows them.

Stories which speak to what we might read into records of different cultures and what we might never know accrue and are hard to resist. Nicolas Rothwell, writing about the increasing production of scholarly books on Australian Aboriginal art, about ethnographic understanding and art scholarship, reminded us that

> the besetting problem for the ethnographic method of interpretation is that much of the beauty it sees and praises is not present on the painted surface but merely implied by it … The fullest comprehension … is reserved for those who are participants, at a deep level, in the ceremonial life of traditional indigenous culture.

Dalrymple's story about the *bopha*'s remarkable memory is not told in order to damn inevitable change and contact. Although it is a poignant example of irrevocable loss, the tape recorder has provided us with a marvellous record of what will change and be lost anyway. Perhaps I am arguing, in food's case, and in particular in Australia, for a slowing down, or for being content not to know everything, for longer mastication before swallowing. Surely this is what good digestion is: a place where experience and language meet and mean the same thing.

The furthest stretch between language and consumption are the advertisements for industrial foods which are of a kind with the new housing estates in my mostly rural patch and which are, against all logical description, called 'The Orchard' and 'The Springs'. In a 1980s novel by the

almost forgotten American writer Walker
Percy, a subversive priest keeps repeating
that words have been 'evacuated'. Like
Michael Pollan, the author of *In Defence of
Food*, I have counted the listed ingredients
in many industrial foods. The tiny package
of cheese spread and three salty biscuits
which is handed out at the hospital where
I give blood is hardly large enough for
the space needed to list the tens of food
additives which ensure its long shelf life.
This disproportionately small mouthful
and long list of 'ingredients' is rather like
the list of credits at the close of a short
film. The best boy might, we suppose, be
offered more work because of his listing;
so too antioxident 304.

It is good that regulations require this list of additives and stabilisers, because it is marvellously off-putting. It is not that they are dangerous but that most of the food in which they appear lacks any flavour which might be associated with real food, and is disconnected from agri-culture. The problem is surely that those of us who shun foods we deem not to be food, and who read labels, have the money and the culinary resourcefulness to choose not to eat them, while those with less income, less culinary education and less choice take the additives, the long shelf life, the depleted flavours and tex-tures, and the relatively low cost, to be a normal diet. With disclosure comes trust, an 'evacuated' word if ever there was one. 'Trust' is also implicit in the acceptance of sealed, sterile packaging. Trust walked out the door some decades ago, away from the kitchen and the soil, and, having been manipulated and orphaned, made a pact with powerful new parents.

Another instance of evacuated words, more contradictory comedy than anything else, was the 'mini apple pie and sultanas treat'—including no sultanas, it required no counting, unlike the seeds of the pomegranate—that was served by an airline. Its packaging boasted that 'We bake fresh every day'. Let's not quibble over adjectives used as adverbs here. On the reverse the smaller print advised that the treat 'can be kept for 6 months if stored at minus 18°C, and if thawed and kept at 5°C will keep for 14 days'.

Choice of food based on knowledge is so central to our wellbeing that you would think it hardly needs another tract by writers like Michael Pollan to point out what the 'market' has done to food in order to make money. In *The End of Food*, Paul Roberts writes, 'Food is fundamentally not an economic phenomenon'. By this I take him to mean that you cannot eat money. Food is sold; money is made; that money is used to purchase something else, centrally food. This is Marxist alienation at its most simple and barren. How old-fashioned, out of kilter with contemporary life, this sounds now, yet I for one am transfixed by the disconnection of food from money, or perhaps I mean the terrible connection food has to money.

Little, obvious things make large points. Recently, at the beginning of winter, shops which sell fruit and vegetables were charging such a high price by weight for lemons (mostly imported, mostly lacking in the quiddity of lemons) that it became unconscionable to purchase them. It is difficult to think of one plate of food which the lemon, either juice or peel, does not improve. The many lemon trees in this area, in front and back yards, in paddocks and leaning over fences, were laden with fruit; there was a luxury of lemons.

Ever utopian, but disconnected and immobilised by a solitary nature, I envisaged a grassroots, unspoken accord whereby everyone with surplus simply put their lemons, and whatever plenty they had harvested, in front of their properties. Used in this way the fence becomes a shelf. The produce would be anyone's for the taking and its distribution a version of gleaning, economic and generous. The Old Testament book of Leviticus includes many troubling laws but sometimes makes sense:

> And when ye reap the harvest of your land, thou shalt not wholly reap the corners of thy field, neither shalt thou gather the gleanings of thy harvest. And thou shalt not glean thy vineyard, neither shalt thou gather every grape of

thy vineyard; thou shalt leave them for the poor and stranger. (Leviticus 19: 9–10)

The poet Mark Doty explained what he meant by love: 'I mean a sense of tenderness towards experience, of being held within an intimacy with the things of the world'. I connect gleaning with love in this sense.

Third Course

However much we read about exotic (that is, not indigenous or locally grown) foods, however much we taste different cuisines and satisfy culinary curiosity, our understanding is shallow compared to that of those who grew up with these foods, the combination of which transforms them into dishes which are then taken for granted as a part of a culture.

In *The Idea of Home*, John Hughes includes a description of his Ukrainian grandmother and his mother cooking in the Hunter Valley in New South Wales and further on writes:

I sometimes wonder whether my first narrative model was not the recipe. The ingredients themselves, particularly to a child, seemed less important than their combination, and the way this combination was always already a transformation, something magical: that the words on the page were connected somehow to the ingredients on the table, but also that these ingredients, when connected, became something else. And the magic went further. For as a child at school I could swap the tiny fragments of my mother's honey cake, of *varenyky* and *piroshky*, for whole cream buns and lamingtons with cream, and with the two things before our eyes, the tiny and the large, my schoolfriends could still consider this an equal exchange. In food I saw early the value of the foreign, and the strange currency of cultural interaction and translation.

I heard Hughes reading extracts from *The Idea of Home*. When he read his own 'I sometimes wonder whether my first narrative model was not the recipe', he pronounced the words as though they had little import, his tone almost dismissive. As its reader I gave this sentence great weight.

Recipes are indeed narratives, storylines, and, as such, essential keys to material culture. We might even go so far as to suggest that particular recipes are so inextricably bound to their place of origin that they become rebuses for an entire culture and its perfecting of nutrition. Working with many different immigrant communities in Melbourne some years ago, watching Iraqi women moulding pounded *kibbe* mixture in the palms of their hands, or Cantonese men and women rolling out wonton circles from a dough they had quickly made, then pleating the thin pastry around a filling with such pretty dexterity, was to sense centuries of unselfconscious practice, of phronesis handed on, of recipes so embedded in the kitchen that they seem never to have needed to be written down, perhaps never were written down. In a book about his family, *Daddyji Mamaji*, Ved Mehta wrote of a household where the women 'learned the knack of making meals without seeming to measure the ingredients'. All cookery involves measurement, and hands make good measures.

The closest a descendant of the first immigrants to Australia might come to this complete knowledge—the sum of practical culinary knowledge of which recipes are a part—is seen in a woman's reply, in a newspaper's food pages, when asked why she douses her Christmas cake with alcohol as it ages: 'Because [my mother] does it, so do I, so I can't tell you what happens if you don't'. This is not far from the *metis* (practical know-how and common sense) of an Iraqi or Chinese cook who does not question the status quo but honours it as part of everyday life. For someone as dyspeptic as myself in regard to the titillating promises that are recipes in books, newspapers, magazines and the web, that woman's repetitive Christmas cake is something of a relief. The cake must be satisfying to the family group and extended community it feeds or the recipe would have been changed.

Recording conversations with women in their seventies, members of the Country

Women's Association, who made a part of a City of Melbourne project called 'Eating the City' in 2004, it was clear that they had spent their adult lives cooking because their families and the people who worked on their farms needed feeding. Cooking wasn't a hobby but labour. Winning prizes for cakes and slices at agricultural shows had been more about the social occasion than the prize, although there was pride in the prize. When asked if their husbands ever cooked, many of them answered, 'He's a good, plain cook'. I puzzled over this as I had interpreted their stories as showing themselves to be just that. Then it became clear that they were saying their husbands can feed themselves if they have to, but that they don't bake, don't make fancy things. This conversation was with a particular generation, and there are many glimpses of change, but the domestic daily meal and the space it is prepared in is the opposite of professional cookery, where men have long wanted to own the creative, egotistical space where cookery is also business.

We have access to an astounding number of recipes. We can tell you, ad infinitum, 'what happens if you don't'. This may be the most accurate way to define what is often touted as an Australian cuisine. The modern, media-celebrated equivalent of the skills shown by domestic cooks in many twenty-first-century Australian immigrant cultures is the professionalism of chefs, cooks who have served a formal apprenticeship and make their living by running kitchens which offer multiple choices to paying diners.

The media pays excessive, fulsome attention to some of these chefs. They have become personalities and their food has become an aesthetic phenomenon. Via magazines, newspapers, their books and television we know their faces and their completed dishes, but there is a void in between. Television provides more evidence of real cooking, but the screen is the ultimate buffer. Television cooks and their comperes tasting a dish and expressing ecstatic satisfaction which falls flat on the glass screen come close to causing offence. Robert Hughes wrote of 'the victory of television over the object of its debate'.

We don't really see these chefs working unless we can afford to go to their restaurants and their kitchen is visible from the dining room, and even then we see only service, which is a stage divorced from preparation and in many ways a compartmentalised and bravura display of juggling at a hot stove, a very different skill from the practical and reasoned decisions about produce, its flavour and its texture, and the possibility of combinations. It is a display of ergonomics and coordinated actions, a skill refined by practice but one which has little to do with what might competently be achieved at home. It has long interested me that when celebrated chefs are asked what they like to eat when not making the food by which their reputation has been made, their answers form a chorus of praise for simple, rustic, cheap or takeaway foods like tripe, phở, laksa, noodles or omelettes.

Competition for diners seems not so much to do with making faultless dishes over and over again but about being seen to be doing something which is always novel and which has the aura of not being able to be repeated by domestic cooks. Often this is true because the preparation involves multiple last-minute garnishes and details that translate into unnecessary chores for a domestic cook. Often the dish seems unfriendly to a domestic kitchen because the plating is so exact, so studied, that it doesn't look like something a table at home might welcome.

The apotheosis of this extreme distance between restaurant and domestic food is the rise of what has been dubbed molecular gastronomy, although it more accurately might be called the cuisine of deconstruction. The popular, simplistic perception of this cooking reduces it to the creation of foams and gels, but it is more exactly the result of science and technical innovation which allows the cook (the technician? the inventor? the magician? the alchemist?) to change the expected texture of a food, to make unexpected combinations, to play games with our naive or traditional culinary preconceptions, to practise sleight of hand. Technical experimentation in the laboratories of multinational companies that produce industrial foods with a long shelf life for wide distribution showed chefs such as the famed and original Spanish innovator Ferran Adrià what might be done in restaurants where the exquisite and ephemeral hold expensive sway.

Grant Achatz, owner-chef of Chicago's Alinea, cooks (a new verb is needed here) dishes such as 'dehydrated bacon wrapped in apple leather' which is then hung from a silver scaffold; 'shrimp, lemon rind, and cranberry-gel tempura fried on a vanilla bean'; and a bean dish which includes a pillow full of nutmeg-scented air. He wants to include aromas as emotional triggers in his dishes, yet the presentation of the almost ridiculously small courses is precise, angular and clickety-clack modern, like a tiny, cool, minimalist interior for the mouth. The combination of the spare and modern with the idea of nostalgia is something of a conundrum. Nostalgia has become a sales pitch. 'I consider what we do an art form,' he says, 'and art is in many ways the opposite of science'. Many decades ago, the Polish gastroenterologist Edouard de Pomiane, who left us with marvellously sensible French cookbooks much praised by Elizabeth David, wrote: 'Art demands an impeccable technique; science a little understanding'.

Words play their part in this fascinating but alienating new cookery, just as they did with the heralded nouvelle cuisine of the 1970s in France. Heston Blumenthal, of the Fat Duck in Bray, England, presents a menu which has included 'sardine on toast sorbet' and 'smoked bacon and egg ice cream'. Achatz names one of his dishes 'hot potato, cold potato'. I have not eaten 'hot potato, cold potato', nor have I eaten Adrià's or Blumenthal's food, not because of any prejudice against their playful, exact artistry (meaning the art of making) but because of the alienation of cost and distance.

Achatz told an interviewer in 2008 that, having worked for Thomas Keller at the famed French Laundry in California, he realised that Keller was 'more interested in what you could do *with* food rather than *to* food', and so he left. This statement has overtones which reach to the torture of espaliered trees and the miniaturising that is bonsai, but Achatz was on his creative way and so to Alinea via a short stint with Adrià. He has invented a dish (more a mouthful) which is a capsule of pressed mango and soy with foie gras inside. 'Mango, soy, foie gras', he told an interviewer. 'Sweet, tart, salty, and fat. You know, it is that easy. That's what people don't understand.'

Sweet, tart, salty, fat. It is as simple as that. South-East Asian cuisine, with the addictive inclusion of chilli heat, has known and presented this combination for centuries, so too Chinese regional cuisines. Molecular gastronomy still keeps to the fundamental dictates of the seduction of our palates. It pays more attention to texture, which we should applaud, and which is one of the great qualities of Chinese cookery. The Chinese have two main words which describe texture: *tsuei* (crisp, crunchy) and *nun* (soft and tender, not fibrous). For instance, 'The skin of Peking duck is fragrant, crisp and rich without being oily (*hsiang, tsuei, yu-er-pu-ni*). Fish balls are at once fresh, crisp and tender (*hsien, tsuei* and *nun*)'. This is taken from the remarkable *Chinese Gastronomy* by Hsiang Ju Lin and Tsuifeng Lin, first published in 1969. *Hsiang* is aroma and *hsien* is the natural, sweet flavour of a food—essential to a satisfying congee, for instance, is the *hsien* of rice. The marvellous, inclusive thing about congee, a gruel of rice or millet, is that it is revered by rich and poor alike. Both know that it is good for the digestion.

Roger Haden, in an essay written after attending a lecture by the physicist Peter Barham (who works with Heston Blumenthal in refining and corroborating the methods used by Blumenthal, and who, make of this what you will, holds the first chair in molecular gastronomy, which is in the Netherlands), claims that molecular gastronomy is 'the cultural expression of a number of interrelated processes: technical innovation, global affluence and influence, individualisation, and identity construction, together with consumer neophilia as this relates to the emergence of new forms of cultural capital'.

Haden's words are a thoroughly contemporary way to write about cookery. No one in the early 1970s, when nouvelle cuisine made its first artful puddle of jus but also made corrections to the culinary ancien régime, wrote about it in sociological terms. This contemporary craze for sleights of hand, for technically adventurous cookery that costs a lot to dine on, for cookery which isn't replicable at home, is not a corrective as nouvelle cuisine legitimately was. Instead, it seems to be, in its motives and advertisement, some version of art via the laboratory. Adrià, for instance, has already produced a three-volume *catalogue raisonné*, which one would normally associate with an artist. The book, according to a Spanish reviewer, is beautiful and practical and 'nothing is kept secret', a generosity lost on domestic cooks.

This very technical cookery is for those of us (and this is most of us) who do not eat at its temples a novel play on culinary word associations, all air to sniff at, like the nutmeg-scented pillow of Achatz's bean dish. Aesthetically it seems to have its origin in the new artistic freedoms of Spain—especially Catalunya, a region which for so long was repressed by Franco's regime—and, connected to this, surrealism and the particular line and draftsmanship of artists such as Dali and Mirò.

In the mid 1990s in Spain, the dishes at restaurants where the food was critically acclaimed were already a far cry from the traditional. You might order a gazpacho as a dessert, a playful transposition more verbal than culinary, which had its origins in nouvelle cuisine. The Spanish high-flyers were already at pains to deny tradition, although there was talk about the peaceful coexistence of the old and the new. This disappoints culinary tourists who want things to stay the same, but until a restaurant becomes so touted that it finds itself in the troubling position of feeding only tourists, it must surely satisfy its local customers, so we might deduce that the affluent Spanish wanted to move on, perhaps to forget. In that same period, we dined on the move with the Spanish by making a meal of tapas—consider the street in Logroño, for instance, where the anchovy, raw and soused, is queen, and another street where blood sausage and entrails are kings.

To dine on tapas is to stretch out a meal. The Spanish food and performance artist Alicia Rios suggested that it is a way of putting off decisions, and once said of her mother that 'she is able to eat yesterday's breakfast the next day or take today's siesta tomorrow'. This endearing, frustrating trait is central to the Spanish psyche and central to tapas, which is one of the most civilised ways to eat and drink and talk in the world, but it cannot be simply copied outside the culture which created it. In part, the new Catalan cooking pays homage to tapas—the progression (without the steps), the small bites. The way of tapas, like the way of tea, has been digested into a particular culture. Haden, in his essay, calls the new cooking a cuisine 'seemingly without culture'—seemingly, nevertheless, connected, but at pains to be at a distance from agriculture and from what went before. By making food that cannot be reproduced by its audience, it makes further claims to be art.

From a distance, this cuisine seems to be admirably consuming for its practitioners, like a new hobby which offers marvellous creative possibilities. On one level, there would seem to be no connection between molecular gastronomy and industrial food and the slippery words that market the latter. The first involves gastronomic knowledge, taste and refined culinary practice, and is the creative conceit of a coterie of talented professional chefs. Its motives are to create ephemeral theatre for the eyes, nostrils and tongue. Industrial food chemists work towards making food uniform and stable. Their science has provided the chefs with the means to a very different end. The paradox might be that the chef who devises a capsule of pressed mango and soy with foie gras inside, or a pillow of nutmeg-scented air, may, in the long run, be more useful to industrial food corporations than to his diners.

Among defenders of the experience of dining on this experimental cuisine with its cool aesthetic are people like the man who said to me, 'I am pluralist about art, about painting and music, I am pluralist about architecture but I am not pluralist about food'. This man has expertise in all that he is pluralist towards, but none in cookery, about which he has strong likes and dislikes. He dines only in the most expensive restaurants, where the service is effusive. In *Libra* Don DeLillo wrote, 'There were times when Larry thought lunch in a superior restaurant was the highlight of Western man'. The pluralist knows, I think, that a superior restaurant is about capital and status but does not know how to dine in any other way.

Main Course

I propose an antidote to restaurants which suspend engagement and which are exclusive because of their price, a manifesto for a different kind of restaurant.

There are no waiters in this restaurant, just as there are no waiters at home. Waiters receive praise and gratitude which is not theirs to receive. They may be a conduit to the kitchen but they also represent a barrier. Their presence distracts the diner from any real connection to the preparation of food. By not employing waiters, this restaurant asks that the diner be involved. I have seen this lack of service work magnificently in the pizza restaurant in the small town close to where I live, although there are in truth some young people who fetch and carry. The diners' involvement in the ordering and delivery of food promotes camaraderie and accidental communication with strangers. It is not work but engagement.

Dining with friends on complicated, sometimes sublime dishes at a famed restaurant, I argued against waiters. One diner was astonished and cried in anguish, 'But we might as well be eating at home!' This is not true, but we have been coerced into believing that service is one of the absolutes about dining out as opposed to dining in, that this is part of what we must pay for. The waiters at this restaurant have been schooled in the exact description of dishes by the kitchen, and they have been trained to attribute the descriptions to the chef himself, as in, '[the chef] likes to say of this dish …' or '[the chef] himself describes this dish as …' These descriptions often overreach, and unless a waiter shows a real performative intelligence about the food the recitation is stilted, verges on the ridiculous and becomes a further test to take before commencing to eat. The printed menu, in which the chef's 'passion' is mentioned, has been pared down to single words, an admirable practice in itself, but the service is verbose.

There will be no choice in this restaurant. The man who cried out at the notion of a restaurant without waiters would no doubt cry out again. At the same time, he chooses to accept the dégustation menu at this restaurant because he is there to eat the chef.

That the chef, his cooks and their apprentices should display their craft by finishing and plating, say, ten dishes at once, is the advertisement of something not entirely to do with cookery. A wide choice is less to do with what the diner might feel like eating, less to do with the modern problems of allergies, prejudices and preferences, than with a different kind of cooking from that which takes place in the home. It is, by misplaced definition, a version of professionalism, when pro-fessionalism is surely to be able to cook consistently good food.

At home it would be a discourtesy to offer a choice, completely out of place.

Why then does it appear de rigueur to offer a choice in a restaurant? To counteract homeliness? And if so, why? When a guest enters your house and you are host, you trust each other. According to Zen Master Joshu, 'there are four positions of host and guest: host as host, guest as guest, host amidst guest and guest amidst host. They illustrate the reality of subject and object'.

In a restaurant, the host is not who he or she appears to be, for surely the host is the cook. The more the diner is objectified—that is, the more distant and commodified the 'trust'—the more the balance of power shifts; the more a diner is alienated from the kitchen, the more the kitchen is disengaged from the dining room, the less the chef feels appreciated, the more the diner sits in judgement.

The restaurant which offers a set menu, a menu which will change logically with supply and season, as well as because of the chef's intermittent and economic need for change and her shifts of imagination, sets up a sense of trust which is far closer to that between friends. 'I am cooking this tonight', the chef says through her straightforward menu. 'If you would like to dine here today, then this is the food.' No restaurant pleases everyone except the one which is situated in a place where there is nothing else to eat and diners arrive at the furthest stages of hunger.

At this restaurant, the food is not plated as individual serves. This too follows the generosity of home cooking. Food placed meticulously on individual plates is 'restaurant' food. At home, there are dishes in the centre of the table and family or guests are encouraged to take from them. We don't lean, nestle or stand certain foods against, next to, or on another food or foods. We cannot do this if we are serving foods which are, for instance, stir-fried or braised. Chinese cookery is in most respects immune from studious presentation, except for the gourmandising Cantonese, who have made a fetish of courtly decoration. The good, agricultural sense of Italian cooking means that it too is immune to picture-making.

The restaurant that offers enough food so that you might help yourself to more, or take a lesser portion to suit your smaller appetite, doesn't plate food in individual portions (and nor do the much more sophisticated cuisines of China and South-East Asia). The generosity is not only in offering dishes to be shared from the middle of the table but also in allowing you to make your own decision about the portions of each part of the dish. Georg Simmel, in *The Sociology of the Meal*, wrote that the circle, the individual plate, is the most isolating shape. We who dine on Western cuisine (and this includes the best modern Australian cooking which, with reform and reason, takes from and tinkers with the traditions of Asian neighbours) have become hostages to the tyranny of portion control, but it is not so much in revolt that this restaurant offers dishes to be shared. Rather it is because this is the most generous, pleasurable and engaging way to dine.

At this restaurant, the diners will pay when they arrive. There is a restaurant in Perth (and others I have heard of in different cities) which asks simply that diners pay what they feel they can afford. The food is Indian and vegetarian, there is no alcohol, and you are welcome to return to the servers and have your plate refilled. Because no price is set on individual plates of food and there are no restrictions on how much you eat, it is possible to pay before eating.

The utopian restaurant would not charge its diners at all, but if I argued for this (even though there are ways to keep feeding people and yet not charge them, one of which is to treat diners as offspring) these modest proposals would not be taken seriously. Instead, all who enter this restaurant will pay exactly the same amount of money, a fair, fixed price which covers everything, and which they pay as they enter, as they would in a theatre or a cinema—or better, say, a gallery where the one donation allows them as much time as they want to spend there.

For the four rural events which composed Plenty for the 2000 Adelaide Festival, and across which we fed some 8000 people, we commissioned bowls from potters who lived in each of the four local communities. By purchasing a bowl those who came to eat were prepared to dine. The price of the food was transferred to the bowl and the bowl was theirs to take home, to be used again and again. Of course, we did not refuse those without bowls. Bread makes a good plate; so too do specific leaves in different cultures. Cupped hands make a bowl—a gowpen, a double handful, was originally the perquisite of grain or flour allowed to the miller's servant. The essayist and poet Octavio Paz has called handmade receptacles 'already sociable'. The Plenty bowls were also a way to make more than just the food local. The potter Damon Moon, who made plates and bowls to be used as the receptacles for all five meals at a food symposium in Adelaide in 2002, wrote:

These are slow pots, organic, variable and sometimes not perfect. They are also regional, made with local ingredients. The clay comes from the foothills to the north east of the city. This area has produced clay for bricks, roofing tiles and pottery since the early days of the city. It is processed from its raw state by Bennett's Pottery at Magill. All the rocks I use in the glazes are also South Australian. The granite and rhyolite which are the main ingredients in the darker glaze come from a quarry between Murray Bridge and Monarto. Other ingredients include talc from Mt Fitton in the northern Flinders Ranges and hand-ground copper in the form of malachite, azurite and chalcopyrite from

Burra, north of Adelaide and Moonta on the Yorke Peninsula. It is very unusual now for glazes to be made in this way. More often they are bought prepackaged: 'just add water and stir'.

By paying before dining, nourishment and the inclusive sense of conviviality stay with us as we leave and are not diminished by the disruption of money. Some will eat and drink more than others, some less. The price of the meal is in fact the price to us all of the upkeep of the restaurant.

The restaurant will be local. In the main, people who eat there regularly will be those who live close by. It might also act as a hub for community meetings and become indispensable to the town in the same way that the local library, now much more than a place to borrow books, has become. The restaurant's intent is not to feed tourists, but there is no shibboleth to sort out who is who. The food used in the kitchen will, as much as is possible, be sourced from local producers, near neighbours with an excess of certain crops, or grown by the cooks. The closest farmers' market will become a pivotal supplier while ensuring that there is always enough produce left for domestic cooks to purchase. The cooks themselves will be locals, and they will ensure that young people who want to work and learn in the kitchen will be local too. A strong case for these ideals has been in place for many years in Russell Jeavons' restaurant in a small town in South Australia. Jeavons even reckoned some years ago that by serving pizza from his handmade oven, and asking that we eat it with our hands, he was saving water by lessening the load for the (human) dishwasher.

The restaurant will be modest in all respects. There will be no cult of personality, and the owners will not collude with the press to allow this to happen. This modesty should not be mistaken for dampened talent. There will be no advertising; word of mouth has most strength locally. The modesty of the restaurant will also apply to its size. In this respect, the example of chamber music makes a good comparison and is not far-fetched. A soloist and an orchestra are playing to an audience. A small group of musicians—a string quartet, for instance—is inviting the audience into the music-making. Chamber music by its nature is lost in a large space, lost when played to a large audience. In a small room where the listeners (diners) are physically close to the musicians (cooks), there is a complicity and a conviviality which are inclusive of both the musicians and the listeners. In Christopher Marlowe's play *The Jew of Malta* there is the line 'And as their wealth increases, so enclose infinite riches in a little room'. Differently, the wealth in this restaurant is the common interest in its wellbeing, the infinite riches those of inclusiveness and engagement. No seat in the house is more privileged than another. With the meal, these seats are around a table, although 'table' need not be taken literally. Michael Symons, author of *The Pudding that Took a Thousand Cooks* and *The Shared Table*, as well as other histories and philosophies of food and culture, has said that he is not a food writer but someone who writes about the meal. This is an important distinction and is inclusive not only of civility and table talk but also of the perfecting of nutrition; digestion takes time.

If all this sounds like family, and like home, or an extension of home, that's the point. By being a place which is nothing like home (waiters, multiple choice, portioned food), restaurants devalue real engagement, and the balance of power is uneven. Is it not enough that the restaurant provides a meal which saves you having to shop, cook and clean up, and might sometimes serve food you would never have thought to cook, and at the same time provides a space in which you have contact with your neighbours and strangers?

Somewhere in the space between the extremes of industrial, supermarket food affordable to most of us and technically innovative, alchemical new cooking in public dining rooms available only to the very comfortably off is a place which requires us to engage with agriculture and to cook for ourselves, a place of good digestion. In 1982, Jean-François Revel, admittedly a Frenchman addressing almost exclusively French gastronomy, closed *Culture and Cuisine* with the

hypothesis that 'the predominant characteristic of contemporary gastronomy,
in these closing years of the twentieth
century, appears to me to be obvious: for
better and for worse, this predominant
characteristic is the return to nature'.
Revel's conclusion is not a vote for noble
savagery. His text is a historical explora-
tion of two streams of cookery, 'silent
cuisine and cuisine that talks too much',
domestic and 'fancy'. He sees a constant
battle between 'the good amateur cook and
the thinking chef, a lover's quarrel that, as
in all adventure novels, ends, after many a
stormy scene, with a marriage'.

The place where good digestion waits
on appetite is one in which everyone,

domestic or professional, who cooks with experience and knowledge particular to their kitchen and culture is equally valued. We have become transfixed by public, commercial dining, as though these kitchens and dining rooms, and only these, might show us who we are. What does Australia digest? Would it not be interesting to include in the census form a question such as 'What did you eat for breakfast and dinner yesterday?'

Petits Fours

Ihab Hassan was born in Cairo in the 1920s. He studied electrical engineering and veered west to America, where another distracting vector found him teaching comparative literature for many, many years and writing many books. Distracted again, he has, in the last couple of decades, written about art and something which might be termed the mystical. His reading is prodigious, his writing lapidary, elliptical, open-ended.

In 1994, he gave the Emmy Parish Lectures in American Studies at Baylor University in Texas. The first begins, 'I must avow, somewhat unfashionably, that the love of literature, particularly of American literature, has been a central fact in my life'. This essay is in many ways a valediction for his life in academe, whose pleasures (including those of reading and literary criticism and friendships) have been eroded by political correctness. It is a late-in-life essay, and it concludes with a list of lovely, contradictory things which Hassan admires, one of which is 'a certain kind of faith, indistinguishable from doubt'.

Hassan's writing and criticism have taught me much about the dangers of didacticism, without effecting any cure. I offer a plate of my own admirations, not too sweet, not so many as to cause indigestion, and, like Hassan's, 'in no order I can discern', for I must avow, somewhat fashionably, that the love of cookery, particularly domestic cookery, has become a central fact in my life.

If a man works beside me in the fields, he can sit beside me at the dinner table.
(a German soldier referring to a French prisoner of war)

Eating is an agricultural act.
(Wendell Berry, *What Are People For?*)

I have three chairs in my house; one for solitude, two for friendship, three for society.
(Henry David Thoreau)

When it came to saying goodbye, the aunt held my hand, and in her eyes there was this same special expression of attention to the moment. If two people are laying a tablecloth on a table, they glance at one another to check the placing of the cloth. Imagine the table is the world and the cloth the lives of those we have to save. Such was the expression. (John Berger, *A Moment in Ramallah*)

When I got home I heard John Barbirolli conducting Beethoven's Seventh Symphony, over the air. What was agriculture for, it seemed to me, except that such a thing as that symphony and the playing of it should be made possible? To make bread so that it shall be possible for mankind to have more than bread and hear the scripture of the kings; to listen to a Beethoven, a Sibelius, a Tchaikovsky, uttering some far message to paradox and joy.

(John Stewart Collis, *The Worm Forgives the Plough*)

I am this world and I eat this world.
Who knows this, knows.
(Taittireeya Upanishad)

Of luxury, the fruit is luxury.
(Henry David Thoreau)

Cuisine is a perfecting of nutrition.
(Jean-François Revel)

Monsieur le Maire, you are, I trust, still dreaming [of] your extensive plan for the rebuilding of the centre of Lyon [and] the demolition of the prisons of St Joseph and St Paul … I would like to make a suggestion. The area the two prisons cover is small. Less than two hectares. Imagine this site turned into an apple orchard ... It would be the first apple orchard in the heart of a city in the entire world!

(John Berger, *The Shape of a Pocket*)

When the Rev. Sydney Smith (1771–1845) was given a parish, he described it as 'deprived' because it was '12 miles from a lemon'. Responding to this 200-year-old plea for the local, a perceptive friend said, 'In this small complaint he addresses time, geography and consumption'.

There is too much food in food writing now—too much food and too little that goes further.

(Adam Gopnik)

If you have a garden and a library you
have everything you need.
(Cicero)

There are now four fruit left on the pomegranate tree, left only because I like to see
them on bare branches, like the persim-
mons left on trees bare of leaves in Japan
in the winter, the fruit of the new year.
One of these pomegranates is now half-
eaten by a pair of Eastern Rosellas. From
A Zen Harvest: 'As if opening its mouth/
Revealing its bowels:/ Pomegranate'. I
watch the marauding birds without shout-
ing them away, just as I have watched a
pair of New Holland Honeyeaters tend to
their exquisite nest built recklessly close
to the front door. Enough fruit has been

used and given away so that I am less disgruntled by the rosellas' version of theft and turn it into end-of-season sharing. There is an old American saying: 'One to rot, one to grow, one for the farmer, one for the crow', but rosella scans just as well. Had I really thought that the pomegranate defeated the birds?

Experience is everything. For many years I ran restaurants where waiters brought food to diners and changed tablecloths. We produced a menu of many dishes and we went along with the food media in making parochial heroes of ourselves. It isn't only that I am much older but that I have now grown food—although never meat, and never aspiring to self-sufficiency. It is not a reversing of position but that digestion is a long and thoughtful process. I had no knowledge then of what now gives pleasure. A different philosophy and practice is now possible.

In his recent book *The Craftsman*, the sociologist Richard Sennett's intention is to 'make the case my juvenile self could not make to [Hannah] Arendt [his pivotal teacher], that people can learn about themselves through the things they make, that material culture matters'. In one section of the book he examines ways to write down recipes, defining Elizabeth David's style as a version of 'scene narrative'. For Sennett, David was attempting to 'impart technique through evoking the cultural context of the journey'. I agree that she was not particularly successful in this, but at her best she was perhaps the supreme plain cookery writer even though she made little attempt to explain technique. Sennett sees David's purpose as jolting the reader 'into thinking gastronomically', which is to say that eating is the last act of a long narrative.

This begins with agriculture, and with inclusive social concerns. Both are excluded from the least sustainable kind of food writing which presumes we learn only from the top down, from 'lazy-luscious-land'. Pure indulgence distracts, insulates and leads inevitably to indigestion. Home cannot always include a space for growing food, but it is where thinking about food makes the most sense. The seventeenth-century Mexican nun Sor

Juana Inús de la Cruz wrote: 'What shall I tell you, my Lady, of the secrets of nature I have learned while cooking? … One can philosophise quite well while preparing supper. I often say, when I have these little thoughts, "Had Aristotle cooked, he would have written a great deal more"'.